What Are Clouds?

by Ellen Lawrence

Consultants:

Suzy Gazlay, MA
Recipient, Presidential Award for Excellence in Science Teaching

Kimberly Brenneman, PhD
National Institute for Early Education Research, Rutgers University
New Brunswick, New Jersey

New York, New York

Credits

Cover, © Kevin Schafer/Minden Pictures/FLPA, and © mamahoohooba/Shutterstock, and © Dim154/Shutterstock, and © XAOC/Shutterstock, and © Valentina R./Shutterstock; 3, © Andrey Armyagov/Shutterstock; 4, © Tyler Olson/Shutterstock; 5, © Andrey Yurlov/Shutterstock; 6, © mates/Shutterstock; 7, © Yuriy Kulyk/Shutterstock; 8–9, © holbox/Shutterstock; 8R, © djgis/Shutterstock; 9R, © cloki/Shutterstock; 10T, © James Steidl/Shutterstock; 10BR, © Margo/Shutterstock; 10BL, © pjorg/Shutterstock; 11, © irin-k/Shutterstock, and © Rafai Fabrykiewicz/Shutterstock; 12T, © Adisi/Shutterstock; 12C, © Ralph F. Kresge/NOAA Picture Library; 12B, © bokicbo/Shutterstock; 13L, © David P. Lewis/Shutterstock; 13C, © serg64/Shutterstock; 13R, © Christophe Testi/Shutterstock; 15TL, © leonid_tit/Shutterstock; 15, © Ingo Schulz/Imagebroker/FLPA; 17, © ImageBroker/FLPA; 17TR, © Steve McCutcheon/FLPA; 19, © Yva Momatiuk & John Eastcott/FLPA; 19TR, © mmm/Shutterstock; 20, © Peter Van Rhijn/All Canada Photos/Superstock; 21, © Can Balcioglu/Shutterstock; 22TL, © Adisi/Shutterstock; 22TR, © Ingo Schulz/Imagebroker/FLPA; 22CL, © ImageBroker/FLPA; 22CR, © Steve McCutcheon/FLPA; 22BL, © bokicbo/Shutterstock; 22BR, © mmm/Shutterstock; 23TL, © serg64/Shutterstock; 23TC, © Yuriy Kulyk/Shutterstock; 23TR, © tr3gin/ShutterStock; 23BL, © irin-k/Shutterstock; 23BR, © leonid_tit/Shutterstock.

Publisher: Kenn Goin
Editorial Director: Adam Siegel
Creative Director: Spencer Brinker
Design: Alix Wood
Editor: Mark J. Sachner
Photo Researcher: Ruby Tuesday Books Ltd

Library of Congress Cataloging-in-Publication Data

Lawrence, Ellen, 1967–
  What are clouds? / by Ellen Lawrence.
     p. cm. — (Weather wise)
  Includes bibliographical references and index.
  ISBN 978-1-61772-404-6 (library binding) — ISBN 1-61772-404-1 (library binding)
  1. Clouds—Juvenile literature. 2. Cloud forecasting—Juvenile literature. I. Title.
  QC921.35.L39 2012
  551.57'6--dc23
                          2011048443

For more information, write to Bearport Publishing Company, Inc., 45 West 21st Street, Suite 3B, New York, New York 10010. Printed in the United States of America in North Mankato, Minnesota.

10 9 8 7 6 5 4 3 2 1

Contents

What Are Clouds Made Of?........4

Water's Amazing Journey 6

Creating Clouds......................8

It's Raining, It's Pouring! 10

Meet the Cloud Families 12

Fluffy Cumulus Clouds.............14

Gloomy Stratus Clouds 16

Icy Cirrus Clouds....................18

Walking Through a Cloud........20

Science Lab............................22

Science Words 23

Index 24

Read More 24

Learn More Online....................24

About the Author 24

What Are Clouds Made Of?

A jumbo jet speeds through the air.

As passengers look out their windows, everything suddenly turns white!

Drops of water stream across the outside of the plane's windows.

What's happening?

The airplane is flying through a huge white **cloud**.

The plane's windows are wet because the cloud is made up of billions of water droplets!

clouds seen from a plane window

How do you think the water that makes up clouds gets into the sky?

A cloud may look fluffy and light, but the water that makes up one cloud can weigh more than a jumbo jet!

5

Water's Amazing Journey

The water that makes up a cloud may have come from the ocean, a pond, a puddle—or all three.

How does water get from a pond or a puddle into the sky?

When the sun's heat warms up water, the water changes into a **gas** called **water vapor**.

This invisible vapor floats up into the air and begins to rise into the sky.

Fill a small clear plastic cup with water. On the outside of the cup, use a pen to mark the water level. Place the cup in a window that gets lots of sun. Check the cup every day. What is happening to the water?

sun

Invisible water vapor rises from the pond into the air.

Some of the water from oceans, lakes, rivers, and ponds is always changing into vapor. The air is filled with water vapor, but it's not possible to see it!

Creating Clouds

High above Earth, the air is cold.

As water vapor rises, this cold air makes the vapor cool down.

As the vapor cools, it changes back into tiny water droplets.

The water droplets stick to bits of dust that are floating in the air.

They gather together with billions of other droplets and form a cloud!

cloud

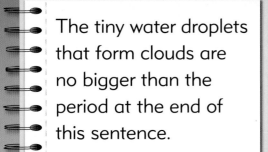

The tiny water droplets that form clouds are no bigger than the period at the end of this sentence.

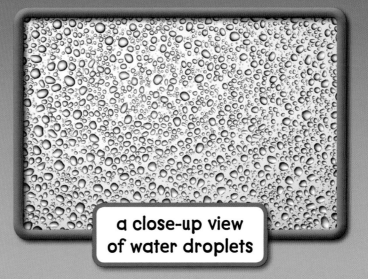

a close-up view of water droplets

In a cloud, the tiny water droplets join together to make larger drops.

When the drops are too heavy to float in the air any longer, they fall from the cloud as raindrops.

If the air around a cloud is very cold, the tiny water droplets may freeze.

They become tiny bits of ice called crystals.

Up to 200 crystals might stick together to make one snowflake!

snowflakes

Look at some clouds. What do you notice about them? How would you describe the clouds you see?

How Clouds Are Formed

3. Water droplets form clouds.

2. Water vapor rises into the air.

4. Rain or snow falls back to Earth.

1. The sun heats up water.

All around the world, clouds are always forming and making rain and snow.

Meet the Cloud Families

Weather scientists use the shapes of clouds to sort them into three main groups.

Cumulus (KYOOM-yuh-luhss) clouds look like puffy white balls of cotton.

Stratus (STRAY-tuhss) clouds cover the whole sky like layers of thick gray blankets.

Cirrus (SEER-uhs) clouds look like white smoke or wispy white feathers high above Earth.

It's possible to tell what the weather will be like by looking at the shapes and colors of these clouds!

cumulus clouds

stratus clouds

cirrus clouds

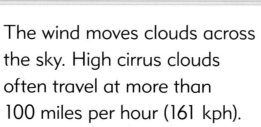

The wind moves clouds across the sky. High cirrus clouds often travel at more than 100 miles per hour (161 kph).

Look at the shapes of the clouds on this page. Which cloud family does each group of clouds belong to?
(See answers on page 24.)

cloud family A

cloud family B

cloud family C

Fluffy Cumulus Clouds

Cumulus clouds normally float less than 6,500 feet (1,981 m) above Earth.

White cumulus clouds in the sky mean there won't be any rain.

When they turn gray, however, it's a sign that rain will soon be falling!

The word *cumulus* means "a pile" or "a heap."

This diagram shows the height of cumulus clouds.

18,000 feet
(5,486 m)

12,000 feet
(3,658 m)

6,000 feet
(1,829 m)

cumulus clouds

White cumulus clouds mean no rain.

Dark cumulus clouds mean rain.

Gloomy Stratus Clouds

It's often hard to see where gray stratus clouds begin and end.

When these clouds are just a few thousand feet above Earth, they produce drizzle.

Drizzle is rain that's made up of very tiny drops of water.

Stratus clouds that form higher in the sky are called altostratus clouds.

Rain or snow falls from them.

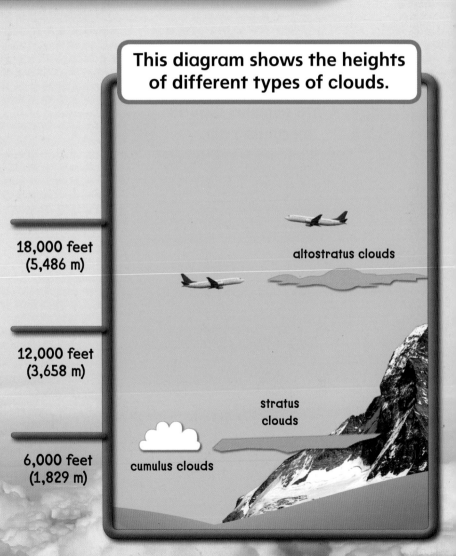

This diagram shows the heights of different types of clouds.

18,000 feet
(5,486 m)

12,000 feet
(3,658 m)

6,000 feet
(1,829 m)

altostratus clouds

stratus clouds

cumulus clouds

stratus clouds

altostratus clouds

The word *stratus* means "a layer."

17

Icy Cirrus Clouds

Cirrus clouds float more than 20,000 feet (6,096 m) above Earth.

This part of the sky is so cold that cirrus clouds are made only of ice crystals.

High white cirrus clouds mean there won't be any rain or snow.

However, if cirrus clouds turn darker and begin to clump together, they are becoming cirrostratus clouds.

Then there will be rain or snow within 24 hours.

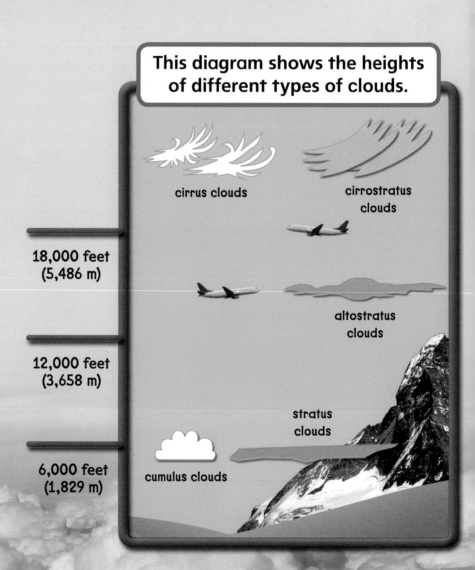

This diagram shows the heights of different types of clouds.

cirrus clouds

cirrostratus clouds

18,000 feet (5,486 m)

altostratus clouds

12,000 feet (3,658 m)

stratus clouds

cumulus clouds

6,000 feet (1,829 m)

cirrostratus clouds

cirrus clouds

The word *cirrus* means "a curl or a ringlet in someone's hair."

What do you think it would feel like to walk through a cloud?

Walking Through a Cloud

Fog is a cloud that is close to the ground instead of up in the sky.

Fog forms when **moist** air close to the ground gets cool.

The water vapor in the air cools down and turns into tiny water droplets.

The droplets then form a cloud that floats close to the ground.

If you have ever walked through fog, you have been inside a cloud!

a foggy day

Fog feels wet and cool and makes it hard for people to see very far ahead.

fog

Science Lab

Be a Cloud Spotter!

The cloud chart shows some clouds you might see in the sky.

It also tells you what kind of weather to expect when you see these clouds.

In a diary, draw pictures of the clouds you see in the sky.

Write the date and record what weather happened that day.

Can you match your clouds to the chart?

Cloud Diary

October 10
gray cumulus cloud

It rained in the afternoon!

Cloud Chart

cumulus clouds (white)
No rain or snow today.

cumulus clouds (gray)
It is likely to rain today.

stratus clouds
There will be drizzle.

altostratus clouds
There will be rain or snow.

cirrus clouds
No rain or snow today.

cirrostratus clouds
Rain or snow is likely within 24 hours.

Science Words

cloud (KLOUD) a mass of tiny water droplets or bits of ice floating in the sky

gas (GASS) matter that floats in air and is neither a liquid or a solid; most gases, such as water vapor, are invisible

moist (MOIST) something that is damp or slightly wet

water vapor (WAW-tur VAY-pur) water that has changed into a gas; water vapor rises and spreads out through the air

weather (WETH-ur) how hot or cold it is outside, and other conditions, such as rain, wind, and snow

Index

air 4, 6–7, 8, 10–11, 20
altostratus clouds 16–17, 18, 22
cirrostratus clouds 18–19, 22
cirrus clouds 12, 18–19, 22
cumulus clouds 12, 14–15, 16, 18, 22
drizzle 16, 22

dust 8
fog 20–21
gases 6
ice crystals 10, 18
rain 10–11, 14–15, 16, 18, 22
shapes of clouds 12–13
snow 10–11, 16, 18, 22

stratus clouds 12, 16–17, 18, 22
sun 6–7, 11
water droplets 4, 8–9, 10–11, 16, 20
water vapor 6–7, 8, 11, 20
wind 12

Read More

Herriges, Ann. *Clouds (Weather)*. Minneapolis, MN: Bellwether Media (2007).

Rockwell, Anne. *Clouds (Let's-Read-and-Find-Out Science)*. New York: HarperCollins (2008).

Saunders-Smith, Gail. *Clouds (Weather)*. Mankato, MN: Capstone (2006).

Learn More Online

To learn more about clouds, visit
www.bearportpublishing.com/WeatherWise

Answers

The cloud families on page 13 are:
cloud family A – cirrus clouds
cloud family B – cumulus clouds
cloud family C – stratus clouds

About the Author

Ellen Lawrence lives in the United Kingdom. Her favorite books to write are those about animals and nature. In fact, the first book Ellen bought for herself, when she was six years old, was the story of a gorilla named Patty Cake that was born in New York's Central Park Zoo.